THE ROMANTIC ERA
Intermediate Level

T0084254

Compiled and Edited by Richard Walters

AUDIO ACCESS INCLUDED
Recorded Performances Online

Recorded by

Elena Abend
Jeffrey Biegel
Alexandre Dossin
Matthew Edwards
Brian Ganz
Stefanie Jacob
Jennifer Linn
Margaret Otwell
William Westney

To access companion recorded performances online, visit:
www.halleonard.com/mylibrary

Enter Code
6969-2456-8061-2062

On the cover:
Clouds (1822)
by John Constable (1776–1837)

ISBN 978-1-4803-3827-2

G. SCHIRMER, *Inc.*

DISTRIBUTED BY

HAL•LEONARD®
CORPORATION
7777 W. BLUEMOUND RD. P.O. BOX 13819 MILWAUKEE, WI 53213

www.musicsalesclassical.com
www.halleonard.com

CONTENTS

Though the table of contents appears in alphabetical order by composer, the music in this book is in progressive order.

The price of this publication includes access to companion recorded performances online, for download or streaming, using the unique code found on the title page. Visit **www.halleonard.com/mylibrary** and enter the access code.

The music in this collection has been edited by the compiler/editor Richard Walters, except for the pieces previously published in other volumes in the Schirmer Performance Editions series:

Burgmüller: Gentle Complaint; Restlessness
from *Burgmüller: 25 Progressive Studies, Opus 100*
edited and recorded by Margaret Otwell

Burgmüller: Confidence
from *Burgmüller: 18 Characteristic Studies, Opus 109*
edited and recorded by William Westney

Chopin: Prelude in E minor; Prelude in B minor; Prelude in A Major
from *Chopin: Prelude*s
edited and recorded by Brian Ganz

Grieg: Arietta; Waltz; Dance of the Elves; Puck
from *Grieg: Selected Lyric Pieces*
edited and recorded by William Westney

Gurlitt: The Little Wanderer; Hunting Song
from *Gurlitt: Albumleaves for the Young, Opus 101*
edited and recorded by Margaret Otwell

Heller: Study in A minor
from *Heller: Selected Studies, Opus 45 and 46*
edited and recorded by William Westney

Schumann: Of Strange Lands and People
from *Scenes from Childhood, Opus 15*
edited and recorded by Jeffrey Biegel

Schumann: Hunting Song; The Reaper's Song; Little Romance
from *Album for the Young, Opus 68*
edited and recorded by Jennifer Linn

Tchaikovsky: The Wooden Soldier's March; Mazurka; Little Neapolitan Song; Sweet Dream
from *Tchaikovsky: Album for the Young, Opus 39*
edited and recorded by Alexandre Dossin

COMPOSER BIOGRAPHIES
AND
PERFORMANCE NOTES

AMY MARCY BEACH

American composer and pianist.
Born in Henniker, New Hampshire, September 5, 1867; died in New York City, December 27, 1944.

Amy Beach (her maiden name was Amy Cheney) was one of the first female composers to be recognized with success in the United States. She composed her first piano piece at age four. Her first published piece came at age sixteen. That same year she made a debut as a pianist with the Boston Symphony. Her many works include the *Gaelic Symphony*, a piano concerto, the opera *Cabildo*, many piano pieces, chamber music, and over 150 art songs. Beach was deeply interested in theory and composition, and translated various treatises from French and German. In 1892 she became the first female composer to have a piece performed by the New York Symphony. After the death of her husband in 1910, she composed and performed for the rest of her life, and was a leading cultural figure of her day. Beach had the condition of synesthesia, a neurological association of color with sound. The five movements of the *Children's Album*, Op. 36, were composed in 1897.

Gavotte in D minor
from *Children's Album,* Op. 36, No. 2

A gavotte was a dance movement in the Baroque Era, generally in 2/2 time, characterized by regular phrasing, binary form, and in a moderate tempo. As a Baroque dance movement, a gavotte was slower than a bourrée, rigadon, or gigue. Composers after the Baroque period used the label "gavotte" vaguely, and virtually none of the Baroque characteristics were retained. Beach probably meant a light dance-like quality for this piece in giving it this title. The first advice to the pianist is to play this music without pedal. The articulation, marked on every note, is generally staccato. Even when it is not staccato, the slurred notes are brief and should be accomplished with the fingers, not the pedal. The composer also has given us quite clear dynamic contrasts, going from ***pp*** to ***f***. Most important is a playful, light touch that the music asks of the pianist. That lightness of touch is not only a matter of volume; even in the *forte* sections there should be buoyancy in the fingers. The form

is ABA and the sections are easily identified. The B section, beginning in measure 17, has a double pedal tone in the left hand throughout, creating a folk-like quality and implying something akin to bagpipes. The tempo needs to be very steady, as in any dance music, including this gavotte. The spots marked "*sopra*" in measures 23 and 38 mean that the right hand crosses the left hand, but just barely. Find the playful mischief in this minor key gavotte.

JOHANN FRIEDRICH BURGMÜLLER

German composer, pianist, and teacher.
Born in Regensburg, December 4, 1806;
died in Beaulieu, France, February 13, 1874.

The Burgmüllers were a musical family. Johann August Franz, the patriarch, was a composer and musical theatre director as well as the founder of the Lower Rhine Music Festival. Johann Friedrich's brother Norbert was a child prodigy at the piano and a composer. Johann Freidrich distinguished himself from his family by leaving Germany and establishing a career in Parisian circles as a composer of French salon music. Later in life he withdrew from performing and focused on teaching. He wrote many short character pieces for his students as etudes. Several collections of these are perennial favorites of piano teachers, especially opus 100, 105, and 109.

Gentle Complaint (Douce Plainte)
from *25 Progressive Studies,* Op. 100, No. 16

This music is a combination of weary discontent and agitation. There is nothing peaceful about it. Burgmüller creates interest in the first few measures by having a long melody in one hand, and a short, agitated, nervous figure in the other hand. The melody passes to the left hand at the end of measure 5 and back to the right hand on beat 2 of measure 7. The sixteenth notes in the left hand in measure 1, and other places like it, are a bubbling murmur, supporting the melody. This requires an independence of hands, of course. The sixteenth-note left hand figure, as in measure 1, needs to be practiced hands alone until it is perfected in evenness and quietness. The piece is through composed, though it feels as if measures

10–13 are a kind of middle section, and measure 14 feels like a return to the spirit of the opening. Notice the long phrases, sometimes over two measures, which will help shape the architecture of your performance. Burgmüller asks for dramatic changes of dynamics in the second page of the music, accumulating in f in measure 14, and then quickly back down to p two measures later. Resist the urge to include any *ritardando* in the final measure of the piece. This is music that disappears without calling attention to its ending.

Restlessness (Inquiétude)
from *25 Progressive Studies,* Op. 100, No. 18

Burgmüller has created a mood of agitation. The challenge in playing agitated music is to capture the mood without pressing the tempo constantly forward. The simple musical tools are staccato chords in the left hand answered by three slurred sixteenth notes in the right hand. This describes almost the entire piece. Notice in measure 7 the left hand chord which briefly departs from the staccato pattern. The sixteenth notes in the right hand need to be absolutely crystal clear in their evenness. The only way to accomplish this is to practice both hands together at a very slow tempo. Gradually, as you master steadiness and evenness, increase the tempo. It will take some experience with this music to play the opening both quickly and quietly. The left hand chords should be practiced alone for crispness. Notice the *subito f* in the second ending in measure 25; the texture of the left hand changes here as the composer asks us to slur rather than play staccato. The form is an ABA plus Coda. The B section begins in measure 9 in the major key; the return of A comes in measure 17; the Coda begins in measure 25.

Confidence
from *18 Characteristic Studies,* Op. 109, No. 1

True confidence is moving forward with quiet self-assurance, and that sureness of motion certainly is characterized in this music. Even though there is busyness created by the triplet figure, the top voice in the right hand and left hand give us quarter notes that move smoothly forward. Try playing the up-stemmed quarter notes only and you will hear clearly the most fundamental structure of the music. The triplets added to that are a rustling decoration. Most pianists will need to diligently practice the triplets in the left hand, which begin in measure 10. Practice hands alone, first at a slow tempo, in order to match the tempo of the right hand triplets that characterize the rest of the piece. (You cannot suddenly slow down just because your left hand cannot play the figure as quickly as the right hand!) The form is ABA plus Coda. The B section is measures 10–17; the A section returns in measure 18. The Coda begins in measure

26. The Romantic qualities of the piece are not only in its harmony, but in the swells of emotion which are indicated in the *crescendos*, *decrescendos*, and dramatic changes to dynamics. One should practice this piece without using any pedal. Pedal should only be added after the music is well mastered. Do not rely on the pedal as a crutch or as a cover for any lack of clarity in your playing.

FRÉDÉRIC CHOPIN
Polish/French composer and pianist.
Born in Želazowa Wola, March 1, 1810;
died in Paris, October 17, 1849.

A major Romantic Era composer for piano, Chopin created a uniquely personal, forward-thinking style, and revolutionized literature for the instrument. He left his native Poland at age 20 after an education at the Warsaw Conservatory, first briefly to Vienna before settling in Paris for most of the remainder of his life. Chopin became a much sought after piano teacher in the French capital, and was part of the lively salon culture, where he preferred to perform instead of in large concert halls. He is reputed to have had an extremely refined, poetic touch as a pianist. He was in chronic frail health through much of his adult life, and died at the young age of 39, probably brought on by tuberculosis. Because of political upheaval, Chopin was never able to return to Poland, and his nostalgic ache for his homeland is a characteristic heard in his music. The 24 preludes were composed between the years 1836–39. In autumn of 1938 Chopin was staying on the island of Majorca with the writer George Sand. After the onset of illness he was taken to a deserted monastery near the town of Palma, where composition was completed for the 24 preludes.

The Preludes

In music a prelude could be one of two descriptions. It might simply be introductory material to something that follows it. Chopin's preludes are not an introduction, but stand alone on their own. However, they follow the tradition of the genre which establishes the key of a piece. This tradition comes from Bach's famous preludes and fugues. Like Bach, Chopin wrote 24 preludes, one in each of the major and minor keys.

Prelude in E minor, Op. 28, No. 4

This is one of the most well-known of Chopin's Preludes. Most would agree that this music is characterized by quiet but disturbed contemplation, briefly rising to a surge of hot emotion, then falling back into resigned but unhappy contemplation. The composer's indication of *espressivo* at the top of the piece invites a performer to arrive at an individual interpretation, and there are many ways to interpret this prelude. The inescapable musical structure is a right hand melody supported by repeated chords in the left hand, which function as an accompaniment. However expressive one might become with the left hand repeated chords and the compelling changes of harmony, a pianist should not forget that the right hand melody must remain the most prominent feature of this music. It is recommended when beginning to learn a Romantic Era piece such as this that one should resist the urge to add romantic interpretation. In early stages of practice it will serve you well to play without pedal, adhering absolutely to strict rhythm. In other words, get the facts straight first before you interpret the facts. If you jump into a deeply felt romantic interpretation immediately without the groundwork of objectively approaching the content on the page, you will likely come up with a messy result. It might feel painful and certainly unsatisfying to practice this piece slowly without pedal, but have the discipline to persevere. Once you have conquered the notes comfortably, then carefully begin to consider where pedaling should be added. The obvious and most important consideration is that the harmonic changes in the left hand chords should be clear. There should be a pedal change each time the harmony changes. There is a contemplative quality to most of this prelude. After all, the principle motive in the opening is the melody dwelling on two notes. In romantic music, it is just as important to be deliberate and exact with dynamics as it is in music of a more objective aesthetic. Even though Chopin invites interpretation with the *espressivo* marking, he clearly intends that the first 11 measures are to be played softly. With the swell in measure 12, he invites more sound. Beginning in measure 13, there is a surge to *f* culminating on the downbeat of measure 17, followed by a quick *diminuendo*. There is a *crescendo* into the deceptive cadence in measure 21. (A deceptive cadence is one in which the harmony resolves in a surprising way.) Chopin's marking of *stretto*, beginning in measure 16, indicates that he intends that the tempo presses forward in this short section, relaxing back to the *tempo primo* heading into measure 19.

Prelude in B minor, Op. 28, No. 6

The left hand plays a single note melody throughout the prelude and the right hand is the accompaniment. The only section in which the right hand might be considered to have taken the melody is the top voice beginning on the third beat of measure 6 through the second beat of measure 8. Except for this, the texture is the same throughout, with the lower voice in the right hand in quarter notes and the upper voice is repeated eighth notes. Sometimes it helps a pianist to find inspiration in imagining another instrument playing the music. In your imagination it might benefit you to think of the left-hand melody being played by a cello. Imagine the richness of a cello playing this melody, and also the legato that instrument would naturally bring to it. This is a through composed piece, essentially compositionally approached as if it were an art song. The minor key and slower tempo contribute to the somber mood. It would not be inappropriate to practice this music hands separately. When practicing the left hand melody only, imagine yourself a soloist with only this line to play. In practicing the left hand melody without pedal, one wants to create a *legato* tone with the fingers only, and also respect Chopin's dynamics, which create an arch from softness, accumulating a little louder in the middle of the phrase, and then dying back down. (This is known as a "hairpin.") It is interesting to note that the only time the right hand is given a hairpin is in measure 8, when the right hand briefly takes the melody. Practicing the right hand alone is a different challenge. Chopin only gives us his intentions with this figure of a quarter note topped by a repeated eighth note in the first measure; those indications with the accent on the beat and slurred could be applied to most of the piece. One often hears different interpretations of this tempo marking. The pianist on the companion recording as a companion to this volume has chosen a true *lento*, sustaining a remarkable mood. Other pianists may need to move the music a little less slowly, but don't make the mistake of many student pianists who play this prelude too quickly, with the result sounding rushed and unconsidered.

Prelude in A Major, Op. 28, No. 7

This prelude is as if a graceful waltz has been put under a microscope, slowed down and contemplated at leisure. It is almost like a wistful, nostalgic memory. The rhythmic structure of each phrase is unvaried. The eight phrases that comprise this short piece are all of the same length. Chopin gives us the indication *p* and *dolce* at the beginning of the music. This requires sweetness and quietness in the tone. The volume increases only at the point of the surprising change of harmony on the downbeat of measure 12. Pedaling is the same for each phrase. Note that the pedal clears for the quarter-note pickup that begins the next phrase. This prelude is a brief piece of loveliness. It would be a great mistake to play it too quickly and thoughtlessly. Though Chopin did not indicate it, a graceful musical choice might be to play a slight *dim.* through the often recurring repeated chords, such as beats 2 and 3 of measure 1 into the next downbeat.

EDVARD GRIEG
Norwegian composer, conductor, and pianist.
Born in Bergen, June 15, 1843;
died in Bergen, September 4, 1907.

Grieg was the great Norwegian composer of the nineteenth century. After childhood in Bergen in a richly musical family he entered the Leipzig Conservatory at age 15, where he was exposed to the major German musicians and composers of the day. He returned to Norway at age 19, and soon became acquainted with Norwegian folk music, which would be the source of inspiration for his individual musical style. Recognition as a composer and pianist led to Grieg's appointment as conductor of the Philharmonic Society in Oslo; he also founded the Norwegian Academy of Music. Through travel and musical connections he became a part of the international music scene of his day, in contact with many major musical figures. Grieg was an excellent pianist, and his piano music shows an idiomatic understanding of the instrument. The *Lyric Pieces* are short character works composed in nine sets from 1867 to 1901. The eight pieces of *Lyric Pieces*, Op. 12 were composed in Copenhagen in 1867. The final set of *Lyric Pieces* was Op. 71, comprised of seven pieces composed in Leipzig in 1901.

Arietta from *Lyric Pieces*, Op. 12, No. 1
An arietta is a short aria for a singer, and this piece is reminiscent of a song. The top note of the right hand is the melody and everything else is a supporting accompaniment. There are three voices: the aforementioned melody on top, the bass note, and the middle voice, which passes from left hand to right. To understand this music, it would not be unwise to play through the entire piece and only play each of the three voices separately. Play only the top note melody, next play only the middle moving voice, and then play only the bass note. If you can see these voices clearly you can begin to put them together. Putting these voices together is the challenge of the piece. The top note melody should always lead. Begin your practice with both hands together, playing slowly. Force yourself to first play without pedal so that you can clearly hear whether you have made each voice a distinct entity. The only time that the flowing middle voice is interrupted is with the chords in measures 10–12 and its counterpart in measures 20–21. Like many Romantic period pieces, this one asks for a gentle, flowing gracefulness from the pianist. Only after you have mastered this should you begin to carefully implement the composers pedal indications. Though Grieg asks the pianist to do some swells of volume here and there, one would not call this restless

music. A performer should guard against an anxious pressing forward in tempo. The entire piece is marked *p*. Some performers benefit from painting a scene in their imagination that seems to match the mood of a Romantic Era piece such as this.

Waltz in A minor from *Lyric Pieces*, Op. 12, No. 2
Grieg is known as a nationalistic composer of the nineteenth century, meaning that through his music he communicated an identifiable character of this native Norway. Not all of his music has this nationalistic quality, but the Norwegian folk influence is strong in this waltz, which has a playful, dance-like quality. The waltz has a form of AABA plus Coda. The sections are clearly identifiable. The melody leads throughout. In the A sections the melody is in the right hand. In the B section the melody remains in the right hand, but crosses under the left hand accompaniment figure. Grieg has given very specific pedaling for the accompanying figure in the left hand, slurring beats on the "and" of 2 and clearing the pedal for beat 3, which is separated. It will take left hand practice alone to execute this articulation and pedaling cleanly. Like most music by master composers, there is detail and information about almost every note. If you pay careful attention, trying to digest all of these clues, you can create a lively performance rather than a dull one. Pay attention to slurs, pedaling, accents, staccatos, and, of course, dynamics. Note the *subito p* on beat 2 of measures 18, 36, and 70.

Dance of the Elves from *Lyric Pieces*, Op. 12, No. 4
One cannot help but be reminded of the most famous fairy music of the nineteenth century, Mendelssohn's *A Midsummer Night's Dream*, which has the same light, minor key, dance-like character as Grieg's "Dance of the Elves." Throughout the piece, one could say that all eighth notes are to be played slurred and all quarter notes staccato. The only exceptions are quarter notes that occur within a phrase in the left hand in measures 7–8, 15–16, 37–38, and 59–60. This piece needs a crisp touch, making the light staccato chords contrast with *legato* slurred notes. As with any quick music, one must begin practice at a slow tempo. Only when you master all of the notes, practicing hands separately and hands together at a slow tempo, should you move onto a quicker tempo. As you learn the piece, your practice tempo should gradually increase. It would be a great mistake to jump into the performance tempo without this preparation. The tempo on the admirable companion recording is quite fast, and may be unapproachable for some student pianists. That is perfectly OK. Whatever your final tempo, the music should have a graceful dance-

like lightness. There should be no pedal used during practice. We strongly suggest that in performance, pedal would only be used in the three places marked. Even these could be optional. Pay close attention to the very explicit dynamic contrasts. Even when playing *f*, such as in measure 17, one needs to retain a buoyant touch.

Puck from *Lyric Pieces*, Op. 71, No. 3

Puck, from Shakespeare's play *A Midsummer Night's Dream*, is head henchman to Oberon, king of the fairies. (Puck is also known as Robin Goodfellow.) He is a mischievous character with supernatural powers. At one point in the play he states that he will "put a girdle around the earth in forty minutes." Puck is usually played by a young male or a woman dressed in male garb. This piece creates a dazzling impression, but it is actually not as hard as it sounds on first impression. Notice that there are no pedal markings except for measures 19–20 and the final phrase. The use of any pedal except in these two spots will smear the texture, which must be explicitly clear. This music is about the contrast between staccato (generally quarter notes) and short slurred phrases (generally eighth notes). The full measure rests, such as measures 17 and 76, are playful indications of Puck's character. Do not rush through these rests. As with all master composers, Grieg has given us many details of articulation and dynamics, all of which must be carefully observed. As with any quick piece, you must practice slowly, first practicing hands separately. Gradually increase practice speed over several weeks of work, moving to a faster tempo only as you master this piece. Grieg's tempo indication of a half note = 176 is extremely fast. If you cannot master this speed, do not worry. Find a performance tempo that captures the spirit of the piece, which you can maintain steadily, and make sure that you do not create a panicky impression even at a quick tempo. Do not make the frequent student mistake of speeding up in a performance of fast tempo music.

CORNELIUS GURLITT

German composer, organist, and pianist.
Born in Altona, February 10, 1820;
died in Altona, June 17, 1901.

Many of Gurlitt's piano works have colorful, descriptive names, which is not surprising after learning of his lifelong interest in art. He studied music in Leipzig, Copenhagen, and Rome, where he was nominated an honorary member of the papal academy Di Santa Cecilia. His brother Louis was a very successful artist in Rome, and Cornelius himself studied painting for a time while living there. Gurlitt worked as a pianist and church organist, and also served as a military band master. He returned to his hometown of Altona, where the Duke of Augustenburg hired him as music teacher for three of his daughters. Gurlitt wrote symphonies, songs, operas, and cantatas, but he is best remembered today for his pedagogical keyboard pieces.

The Little Wanderer (Der kleine Wandersmann) from *Albumleaves for the Young*, Op. 101, No. 12

Even though it is more complex than a simple three part form, it feels in three large sections. The first section is until measure 25; the next section is the complete change of texture in measure 26; the return of the music of the opening is in measure 41. There is a carefree character to the music. Imagine a traveler happily humming on his or her way. Be careful not to take this Allegretto too quickly. Play the first large section (measures 1 through 25), and its reprise (measures 41 to the end) with graceful attention to phrase. The touch and texture of the middle section (measures 26–40) is completely different, with *f* staccato chords, which must be attacked robustly but very accurately. Notice that the composer has marked the downbeat of measure 29 with an accent. Even though Gurlitt has indicated *f* at the beginning of this middle section, he asks for *crescendos*. You might want to reserve a little volume so that these *crescendos* can be effective. The happy traveler has perhaps encountered some stormy weather in this section, but it subsides, and he or she goes merrily on along with the return of the opening music.

Hunting Song (Jagdstück) from *Albumleaves for the Young,* Op. 101, No. 19

There is a long tradition of imitating bugle sounds in music, whether in the hunt or military references. Particularly in the nineteenth century, portrayals of hunting were not uncommon in music. Gurlitt's hunting song is a giddy, happy event. You can easily hear the high spirits of the hunters and the gallop of the horses. Hunting calls are normally broken arpeggios, simply outlining a chord, such as in the opening E-flat harmony (the traditional "hunting key"). The first technical challenge is the repeated chords in measure 7. You will need to find some bounce on these chords so that your hand or wrist does not become rigid. The piece is a pleasure to play and without a great deal of technical obstacles. It sounds harder than it is, which can be fun. The syncopation beginning in measure 24, with the right hand anticipating the downbeat in the left hand, is not particularly difficult after you find your bearings. Adhere to strict rhythm in this section. It is fun to imagine what Gurlitt meant by the *crescendo* and *accelerando* in measures 35–39, followed by the long rest with a fermata. Did he have some climax of the hunt in mind, followed by the murmuring music heading into measure 41? In measure 52, the treble chords are marked with the left hand to play the lowest note. A pianist could play this chord with the right hand only, but it is more fun to play with both hands. This also prepares the pianist for what is to come in measure 57. Heading into measure 57 is one of the trickiest spots in the piece and will benefit from slow practice, hands separately. This entire piece could be played with no pedal. One might add touches of pedal here and there, but they should be discreet and infrequent.

STEPHEN HELLER
Hungarian pianist, composer, and teacher.
Born in Budapest, May 15, 1813;
died in Paris, January 14, 1888.

Heller begged his parents for piano lessons as a child. At the age of seven he was already writing music for a small band his father put together for him. The boy was sent to Vienna to study with Carl Czerny, but quickly found the lessons too expensive and instead studied with Anton Halm, who introduced Heller to Beethoven and Schubert. At the age of 13, Heller was giving concerts in Vienna as a pianist and two years later began touring Europe. His travels brought him in contact with Chopin, Liszt, Paganini, and most importantly Robert Schumann, with whom he developed a life-long friendship. Heller even contributed to Schumann's journal *Neue Zeitschrift* under the pseudonym Jeanquirit. After two years of touring, the rigorous schedule became too much for the boy and Heller settled first in Ausburg, and then in Paris to teach and compose. He wrote several hundred piano pieces, of which the short character pieces from opuses 45, 46, and 47 are frequently performed today.

Study in A minor (The Avalanche)
from *25 Melodious Etudes*, Op. 45, No. 2
This is one of the most famous of Heller's works and also one of the most well-known student piano pieces. It is interesting to note that the "avalanche" does not begin with downward movement, but upward movement. Perhaps Heller had in mind the frenzied running away from the sudden avalanche. The most characteristic musical gesture is the three-note slur in the left hand then in the right hand. This gesture is repeated again and again, whether going up or down. A technical challenge is to play the three notes in the left hand answered by the three notes in the right hand evenly. Listen very carefully to hear the notes are all of the same duration. Every piece of music needs careful fingering, but a piece such as this, with hands crossing and answering one another and changing register, requires especially careful attention to fingering. The first section is measures 1–16;

section two is measures 17–32; the third section is measures 33–48; the next section is measures 49–72; the last section is measures 73–end. Each of these sections ends with a change in musical texture. Many students question what it means when you have staccato notes slurred, such as in measures 13–14. To get a feel for what the composer intends, first play the notes with short staccato and no slur. Then, instead, play them with no staccato as four notes slurred together. Then just slightly separate them, retaining the intention of the slur but with separation. There is a great deal of drama in this brief piece. After all, an avalanche is a dramatic event! We strongly recommend no pedaling under the eighth-note triplet figure.

THEODOR KULLAK
Prussian/German composer, pianist, and teacher.
Born in Krotoszyn, September 12, 1818;
died in Berlin, March 1, 1882.

One of the most influential piano teachers of the nineteenth century, Kullak began giving concerts at age eight, with the official support of the royal family of Prussia, and met with enthusiastic reception when performing for other royal courts. After briefly studying medicine in Berlin he moved to Vienna, where he studied with Carl Czerny. At the age of 25, he began to work for the Prussian court as a music instructor, and specialized in teaching royal children and youth for many years. He co-founded what would become known as the Stern Conservatory in Berlin, as well as the Neue Akademie der Tonkunst, which became the largest private music school in the country. Through this school Kullak directly influenced thousands of pianists, including Hans Bischoff, Moritz Moszkowski, Xaver Scharwenka, and Nikolai Rubenstein. Kullak's musical output was vast. Writing almost exclusively for the piano, he produced over 150 works, most of which were for students.

On the Playground
from *Scenes from Childhood*, Op. 62, No. 4
If you have spent diligent time practicing your scales, so that you can play nimbly and with agility, here is a piece that will reward you. It will show off the skills you have acquired. Certainly Kullak has captured a playful spirit. Nothing but happy times occur on this playground. Playfulness in music is communicated by clear articulation and intention. One would not find a playful spirit by playing this music with laborious finger strength. Imagine the various games and equipment one encounters on a playground. A common type of play is to twirl, and the first phrase of the piece is like a child having fun twirling, first

quickly and then slowing, eventually coming to a stop. The only held note, in measure 3, might almost mean that moment when you recover from your dizziness and regain your bearings. When we move to the second section, which is on the second page, first the left hand plays a repeated chord that functions as a pedal tone. When it comes around again, it is an octave lower. There should be no pedal used in playing this piece.

Grandmother Tells a Ghost Story
from *Scenes from Childhood*, Op. 81, No. 3
When a grandmother tells her grandchildren a ghost story, it is not likely to be one of true terror. After all, that would give the children nightmares. A loving Grandmother tells such a story with a wink in her eye so that the children know that there is something playful going on. It is entertainment to tell a story. One might call the mood of this piece spooky, on a lighter side of Halloween. This playfulness is communicated with careful articulation. Kullak has marked an articulation on nearly every note of the piece, whether it be slurred or staccato. Sometimes the hands are playing different articulations at the same time. You will not be playing Kullak's composition if you do not execute the articulations as he composed them. They are as essential to the composition as the notes and rhythms. Playfulness is also communicated with the dynamics. It is quite fun to move from *f* quickly to *p* in measures 16–19. Though the composer does not mark it as such, with the return of the opening material in measure 23 a pianist might consider playing even softer than the opening. The trills in the left hand of measures 32 and 34, and particularly in measure 40, will take careful practice and preparation. The composer seems to have a narrative in mind, even if it is an emotional narrative without a specific story. Why else would there be the *f* held note in measure 36, or in measure 44? If you are an imaginative player, you might even invent your own ghost story to follow the emotional narrative that the composer has created. The composer's wit comes through when he tells us as the music trails off in measure 54 that grandmother has fallen asleep. (This is Kullak's note in the score.) After she falls asleep, the children know the story so well, having heard it many times before, that they finish it for her.

EDWARD MACDOWELL
American composer, pianist, and teacher.
Born in New York City, December 18, 1860;
died in New York City, January 23, 1908.

Edward MacDowell showed talent at the piano from an early age. At 16 his mother took him to France to study at the Conservatoire de Paris. He continued his studies in Germany, where he met and performed for Franz Liszt, who encouraged the young composer. MacDowell married and in 1888 returned to the United States, settling in Boston. In 1896, the year *Woodland Sketches* was composed, he became professor of composition at Columbia University in New York. MacDowell was fundamental in building the music program at the school. He retired in 1904 following a buggy accident that gradually reduced his mental and physical health until his death. The MacDowell Colony in Petersburg, New Hampshire, was established in his honor for artists to find inspiration and solitude. MacDowell is often cited as the first American composer to gain stature and success in the European dominated classical music of his era.

To a Wild Rose
from *Woodland Sketches*, Op. 51, No. 1
"To a Wild Rose" is MacDowell's most famous piece. (It can be heard as background music in several Hollywood movies of the 1930s and 40s.) MacDowell has captured the open-hearted simplicity of nature in this music. Imagine taking a walk and coming up on a single, perfect wild rose in a meadow. Such a discovery makes one stop in wonder. The piece is a long gaze at that delicate flower, and a drinking in of serenity. This music is essentially a song, with a melody in the top note of the right hand. In song-like compositions one wonders if the composer imagined a text when writing the melody. Occasionally the left hand briefly answers the melody, such as in measure 14, or in measures 21 and 23. One thing that keeps the piece from being too precious is its colorful harmonies. Notice the artful change in measure 12, comparing it to measure 4. This piece is all about phrasing. Frankly, if you have not developed a sense of sensitive and graceful phrasing, your performance will be dull. Pedaling is also important in this music. Experiment by playing with no pedal, and then a light addition of pedal. If you do choose to use pedal, make sure you make a pedal change when there is a change of harmony in the left hand. There is room for interpretation regarding the tempo. Take caution not to perform at a tempo that is too slow. This music requires a gentle, refined *legato* touch. The composer only takes us to *f* once and it is only briefly in measure 25. It helps some musicians to think of a basic emotion when playing programmatic music. While it might put some pianists off, others will find if they can conjure a feeling of love, it will be the right mood in playing "To a Wild Rose."

CARL NIELSEN
Danish composer and violinist.
Born in Sortelung, June 9, 1865;
died in Copenhagen, October 3, 1931.

Trained as a violinist from an early age, Nielsen entered the Copenhagen Conservatory in 1884, where he continued the study of the violin as well as composition. After graduation he performed as a freelance musician until he was able to secure a position in the second violin section of the Royal Theatre orchestra, one he would hold for sixteen years. On a tour of Europe he met and married Anne Marie Brodersen, a sculptor of some renown. The couple settled in Copenhagen in 1891, where both artists were able to work. Nielsen continued to compose, played in Royal Theatre orchestra, and occasionally conducted. His steady publishing of works eventually earned him a post at the Copenhagen Conservatory teaching theory, composition, and violin. His fame grew throughout his life. He became especially well-known outside Denmark after his death for his symphonic works, though he wrote in nearly every genre, including short piano pieces in a folk style. Five Pieces, Op. 3, were composed in 1890.

Folk Melody from *Five Piano Pieces*, Op. 3, No. 1
Much of folk music is strophic, a term that means different words are sung over the same music in succeeding verses. Nielsen takes a strophic approach to this folk melody. The song seems to be presented in its entirety through measure 12. Measures 13–20 are a repetition of measures 5–12, except for the addition of an imitative tenor voice that answers in canon. At measure 21 we return to the music of the opening. Measure 25 is a Coda in which Nielsen moves to the parallel major key. This piece might be an original composition imitating a folk style, or it might be an art music composition based on an actual folk melody. The composer indicates that the beginning should be "like a hum." This conjures ideas of a group of people singing. The pianist on the companion recording has chosen a tempo that is quite slow, and sustains interest quite well, but here is room for interpretation. This andante could be interpreted as faster. Whatever tempo you choose, make sure it remains steady and regular. This is a song-like composition and the top line melody is always most prominent. When there is movement in the inner voice, pay careful attention, such as in the alto line in the first measure. Create voice leading, meaning moving through the alto line into beats 3 and 4 with some melodic direction and *legato* movement.

MAX REGER
German composer, organist, and teacher.
Born in Brand, March 19, 1873;
died in Leipzig, May 11, 1916.

Reger's father, an amateur musician of some talent, was the boy's first teacher. Soon Max was studying piano and organ privately, and by the age of sixteen was playing organ for church services. Composer Hugo Riemann became aware of Reger's compositional talents. Reger was Riemann's student and followed him to the conservatory in Wiesbaden. After completing his education he served the required year of military service before teaching privately and composing. Reger moved to Munich in 1901, continuing to compose, concertize as a pianist, and teach, until he was offered a position at the Munich Akademie der Tonkunst. In 1907 Reger became the director of music at the University of Leipzig, and subsequently professor of composition, a post he held until his death. Adding to his list of responsibilities, Reger accepted a court position in Meiningen. This rigorous schedule, along with an alleged life-long struggle with alcoholism, led to a premature death. The *Album for Young People*, Op. 17 *(Aus der Jugendzeit)* was composed in 1895.

The Dead Little Bird
from *Album for Young People*, Op. 17, No. 4
Max Reger's music has chromaticism characteristic of German Romantic composers of the late nineteenth century into the early twentieth century. The harmony oozes along with wonderfully colorful and surprising changes. One would best get a feel for this rich harmony by playing this piece slowly using *legato* fingers without pedal. This exercise would reveal the beautiful voice leading in the composition, which occurs in all voices. You will probably add pedal for the performance, but in the practice session you can achieve *legato* phrasing without pedal. It is obviously a sad event for a child to come upon a dead bird. This music captures the empathy and reverence in that sadness, as well as a sense of somber wonder at death. Even though the notes are quite simple, this composition asks for mature musicality from the pianist to build beautifully constructed phrases. Try practicing so that the phrase has a point of accumulation, to which it builds and from which it relaxes. This phrasing should not be exaggerated, however. The tempo on the recording is one interpretation that is certainly valid. As with any tempo, there is room other choices. One might imagine this *andante espressivo* at a slightly quicker pace.

ROBERT SCHUMANN
German composer.
Born in Zwickau, Germany, June 8, 1810;
died in Endenich, Germany, July 29, 1856.

One of the principal composers of the Romantic Era, Robert Schumann's short creative career gave the world major repertoire in symphonies, art song, chamber music and piano music. Besides being a composer, Schumann was an accomplished writer about music, especially as a critic then editor of the influential *Neue Zeitschrift für Musik*. He was married to concert pianist Clara Wieck, who championed his works after his death in 1856, the result a severe struggle with mental illness. Schumann was an early supporter of the young Johannes Brahms. *Scenes from Childhood*, Op. 15 (*Kinderszenen*) was likely composed in February of 1838. Schumann originally composed thirty pieces for the set, but discarded many in reaching his final choice of thirteen pieces. These are adult reminiscences of childhood. The *Album for the Young* (*Album für die Jugend*), a collection of 43 short piano pieces, was composed in the same year for Schumann's three daughters. Schumann made a specialty of short character pieces for piano, not entirely unrelated to his distinctive work as a major composer of art song.

Of Strange Lands and People
(Von fremden Ländern und Menshcen)
from *Scenes from Childhood*, Op. 15, No. 1
This is one of Schumann's most famous piano pieces. The title "Of Strange Lands and People" implies dreamy imagination of places far away. The music is constructed in three voices. The treble melody is the top note in the right hand. (This voice is supported by an alto harmony underneath it in measures 9–12.) The second voice is the bass line, single notes throughout, the lowest note in the writing. The third voice is that of the moving triplets. There also is an implied fourth voice, which is the first note of the triplet figure in measures 1–8 and measure 15 to the end. To understand the piece thoroughly, it is highly recommend that you play each voice separately. Play only the treble melody, next play only the bass line, and then play the treble and the bass together. Then play only the moving triplet voice, noting the voice leading in the first note of the triplet. When you put all the voices together, the music should have a graceful flow. Notice Schumann's phrase marking; for instance, measures 1–2, 3–4, and then a four-measure phrase. As you master this, you will want to make the treble melody slightly pronounced. This composition is similar in character to Schumann's many songs for voice and piano. Play the top line melody with *legato*, as if a singer were singing this melody. Force yourself to practice at a slow tempo without pedal so that you can hear evenness, gentleness of touch and phrasing. Only add pedal when you have mastered the piece to some degree. Pedaling in this case should probably change each time the harmony changes, which most often is on the half measure. The most musically sensitive part of the piece is moving away from the fermata in measure 14. The two eighth notes after the fermata require finesse and insight, otherwise, they will sound awkward. Notice that Schumann has given us primarily a quiet piece marked *p* throughout, with occasional swells in dynamics. The swells should only lead to something around *mp*. The composer apparently gave this piece no tempo marking. The artist on the companion recording gives a good suggestion for a performance tempo, which is graceful and sensitive. Too often, one hears a student pianist play this piece too quickly and too loudly, destroying the wistful dreaminess of this delicate music.

Hunting Song (Jägerliedchen)
from *Album for the Young*, Op. 68, No. 7
Schumann's piece captures the high spirits of a hunting party, echoing the bugle calls and conjuring the horse's gallop. It is a tricky little piece. The first thing a pianist should notice is the differences in articulation at the beginning. First we are asked to accent the principal notes on the beat, followed by a section of arpeggiated notes played staccato. Even though Schumann did not give us a different dynamic for the staccato phrase, he restates the *f* after it, which implies that the pianist should probably lighten up for the staccato notes. Accomplishing the contrast between the horn call accents and the crisp staccato notes is the first technical challenge of the piece. This continues beyond the first phrase. Measures 17–20 are the trickiest in this short piece. Some pianists might find it easier in measures 18 and 20 to play the alto voice E in the left hand, so that the right hand is only playing single notes. The quick changes of chords in measures 21–23, and again in measures 25–27, require great care. One wants to continue the boisterous spirit, but accuracy is paramount. In this edition, we have indicated pedaling in three spots only. We encourage you to carefully consider playing the remainder of the piece without pedal. The playful quality of the hunt also comes through in the sharp dynamic contrasts, moving at times from *ff* to *p*, back to *ff*, then *p*. Like any music at a quicker tempo, this piece requires slow practice, hands alone in the beginning, then slow practice with hands together, gradually increasing the speed as you master the music. Your final tempo should move along, but sound as you are in control of the music, rather than a tempo that is out of control. Playing a piece faster than you can manage will create an impression that you are atop a runaway horse that cannot be controlled.

The Reaper's Song (Schnitterliedchen)
from *Album for the Young*, Op. 68, No. 18

Swinging of the scythe is field work that has a rhythm about it, and Schumann captures the spirit of that work with rhythm in 6/8 meter. He also adds a folk-like quality by adding the double pedal tone at the beginning. This reaper seems to be quite happy at work, and he or she does it with a light touch. The form of the piece is interesting and quite complicated. We begin with a phrase that is repeated; it is answer by phrase B, which is repeated. Then another phrase A, followed by section C, which begins in measure 14. The texture changes completely for the next eight measures. At measure 21, we have A^1, which is a transposition of A up a fourth. This is followed by a transposition of phrase B, also up a fourth, in measures 25. The final eight measures are new material, functioning like a Coda. Voicing is a paramount component of the "Reaper's Song." In phrase A, the melody is the top note in the right hand, accompanied by chords in the other voices. In phrase B, the melody moves to the alto voice (the lower voice in the right hand), which is the same melody we heard in phrase A, transposed to a different key. Notice Schumann's phrase markings. With the melody leading, create the two-measure phrase in measures 1–2, 3–4, etc. Notice that the phrase structure changes in measure 14, where the composer asks us to play longer phrases of four measures. The arpeggiated notes in this section need to be played smoothly. However, in practice, one might begin by playing each note very distinctly at a slow tempo. Contrast that with a smooth playing as you master this music. Notice that Schumann uses an ABA scheme in terms of dynamics. The entire piece is to be played gently and softly except for the middle section, which is marked *f*. The texture changes for the final section, beginning in measure 29, with staccato markings, the first we have encountered in this piece. One could play this entire piece without pedal; we strongly recommend that practice be without pedal. The admirable tempo on the recording is probably as fast as anyone should attempt to play this song. A gentler tempo is also possible.

Little Romance (Kleine Romanze)
from *Album for the Young*, Op. 68, No. 19

Schuman was one of the great lieder composers. His character pieces for piano are closely related to his art songs for voice and piano. This "Little Romance" is quite similar to a melody that would be sung by a singer. We can only guess that Schumann had in mind a little romance that did not exactly end happily. However, it is not the kind of devastating tragedy that befalls some lovers. One gets the impression that whatever has happened, sad as it might be at the moment, things will quickly move on. In measures 1–4 and in other similar places, the musical challenge is playing the melody in both hands together, and accompanying the melody in both hands as well. The melody should slightly lead. To master this you need to practice both hands separately, and slowly. You might also play only the melody with hands together, and then only the accompaniment chords hands together as you identify the elements of the music and isolate them. Notice that Schumann has marked a swell with a *fp* in the middle twice in the first phrase. The bright chords that come in leading into measure 6 change the texture completely. The dynamic also changes drastically to *f*. When you have big chords, such as those in measures 6–7 and 11–12, make sure that all the notes go down together exactly. The piece should generally be played without pedal with the fingers executing the *legato*, except for the few spots where pedal is suggested. The tempo on the companion recording moves along convincingly. One can imagine an acceptable tempo that is not quite so fast. Dynamic contrasts are quite important. It is common to feel dramatic sudden changes of emotion when dealing with romantic troubles. These dynamic changes are key in creating the mood.

PYOTR IL'YICH TCHAIKOVSKY

Russian composer.
Born in Kamsko-Votkinsk, May 7, 1840;
died in St. Petersburg, November 6, 1893.

Tchaikovsky is the great Russian composer of the nineteenth century who achieved the most international success, and whose symphonies, ballets, operas, chamber music and piano music continue to be a central part of the repertoire. Of his piano works, *The Seasons*, Op. 37bis, *Album for the Young*, Op. 39 and his concerto are most familiar to present day pianists and teachers. *Album for the Young* was written in four days in May of 1878, with revisions later that year before publication in October. It was during this year that Tchaikovsky left his teaching post at the St. Petersburg Conservatory and began composing and conducting full time, a move made financially possible by the patronage of Nadezhda von Meck. Much of *Album for the Young* is inspired by folksongs, capturing observations and experiences from childhood in 24 fanciful miniatures.

The Wooden Soldier's March
from *Album for the Young*, Op. 39, No. 5

Notice that Tchaikovsky keeps this march of toy soldiers in the treble range of the piano, which is appropriate for these tiny figurines. A true soldier's march of men in battle would have far more weight than this. This toy soldier's march is not far removed from the march in *The Nutcracker* by the same composer. The military aspect is captured by crisp, steady rhythm that should be very exactly executed. There is no need for pedal in any part of this piece. The toy aspect is captured also by the soft dynamic that Tchaikovsky has given to us. (Small toys do not have enough size to create a louder presence.) The articulation that the composer has given us is a perfect map to create an effective performance. Observe the contrast between the short eighth notes and the slurred, short phrases. A brief military trumpet call occurs in measures 8, 16, and 40. The form of the piece is essentially ABA. The B section begins in measure 17. The texture changes slightly in this middle section with half note chords. The A section returns in measure 33. We recommend no *ritardando* at the end of the march.

Mazurka in D minor
from *Album for the Young,* Op. 39, No. 11

A mazurka is a Polish folk dance in triple meter, slower than a waltz, in which each beat is distinctly heard. Chopin developed the mazurka to a high art form. Tchaikovsky's piece is much simpler than a Chopin mazurka, and closer to the mazurka's folk roots. The accents that Tchaikovsky includes add to its dance-like, folk quality. A master composer such as Tchaikovsky usually gives explicit detail in articulation that, if followed carefully and insightfully, will create a stylish result. Too often pianists do not pay close enough attention to these integral indications from the composer, which are as much a part of the music as the notes and rhythms. A fundamental characteristic appears in the first four measures, with a staccato on the downbeat followed by the next two slurred notes. The left hand throughout this piece is an accompaniment to the right hand melody. The only places where the left hand becomes interactive are in measures 16–17, and measures 50–51. These places are probably the trickiest in the piece. An accompaniment should be somewhat in the background of the melody. Tchaikovsky's articulations are so precise and intricate that they could be blurred and destroyed by unconsidered pedaling. Touches of pedal should only be added briefly and occasionally. One such possibility is pedaling from beat 3 in the first measure to beat 1 in the second measure, and in similar places. Staccato notes in this piece are a sign to use no pedal. Tchaikovsky has given us a careful map of dynamics that contrasts shifting suddenly from *mf* to *p* in measure 5, then a slight swell from *mf* in measure 9, and then a sudden drop to *p* in measure 19, etc. Pay close attention. Interpretation of tempo is subjective. One can imagine an acceptable tempo that is not as quick as on the companion recording.

Little Neapolitan Song
from *Album for the Young,* Op. 39, No. 18

The key to this piece is the word "song" in the title. You will notice that Tchaikovsky has written an accompaniment figure in the left hand throughout under a single note melody in the right hand. There are two large sections to the piece, the second beginning with the fast, flashy finale. This pure Italian melody, with simple accompaniment chords, is characteristic of popular song in Naples. It is highly recommend that one practice hands alone. It might seem boring to practice the left-hand accompaniment alone, but you must do this to make the chords even and crisp. Note that in measure 5 the left hand is always staccato. Regarding the left hand in the fast section, the most challenging spots are measures 41–42 and 49–50. This requires a quick rocking of the hand to go from the lowest note to the top note of the chord. Besides practicing the left hand alone, one should also practice the right hand alone to create a vocally inspired phrase. Tchaikovsky has given explicit details about articulation, indicating which notes are staccato, slurred or accented. The fast section at the end needs slow practice hands alone, and then slow practice hands together. The biggest technical challenge is the repeated notes, which occur in measures 39–42 and again in measures 47–50. Try the recommended fingering of alternating fingers on these repeated notes. You should practice the right hand alone quite a lot to master this, and only gradually increase the tempo as you practice. The final section should sound like a carnival celebration, not an out of control wild ride. (These melodies also appear in Tchaikovsky's orchestral work *Capriccio Italien.*)

Sweet Dream
from *Album for the Young,* Op. 39, No. 21

This is a simple song-like form, ABA, with the B section as measures 17–32. The melody is prominent throughout, first in the right hand in the A section, and then in the left hand in the B section. The texture of the A section is three voices, with the bass line moving in contrary motion to the right-hand melody. The offbeat chords are the middle voice, the accompanying texture. In the B section, the middle voice disappears for a time until the right hand answers almost in quasi-canon to the left hand in measures 22 and 30. In a Romantic period composition, when a composer states "with much feeling," it is an invitation to the performer to bring interpretation beyond what can be notated in the score. In other words, in Romantic Era music, it is simply not possible in music notation to write down all the details of expression which are part of the style. The beautiful recorded performance on the companion recording is one excellent interpretation of what Tchaikovsky meant by "with much feeling." You will notice nuances and phrase shape and very slight *rit.* here and there that help the piece come alive. This music is full of sincerity. One should guard against it coming across in any way thoughtless or unconsidered.

—Richard Walters, editor
Joshua Parman, assistant editor

Gavotte in D minor
from *Children's Album*

Amy Marcy Beach
Op. 36, No. 2

Fingering is from the first edition.

The Reaper's Song
(Schnitterliedchen)
from *Album for the Young*

Robert Schumann
Op. 68, No. 18

Edited and with fingering by Jennifer Linn.

To a Wild Rose
from *Woodland Sketches*

Edward MacDowell
Op. 51, No. 1

With simple tenderness (♩ = 88)

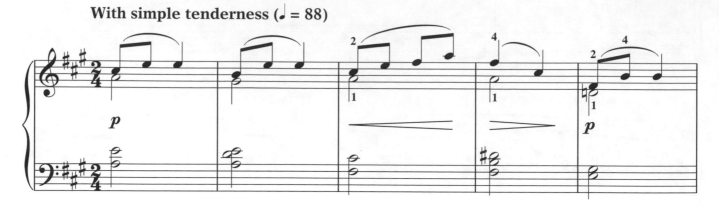

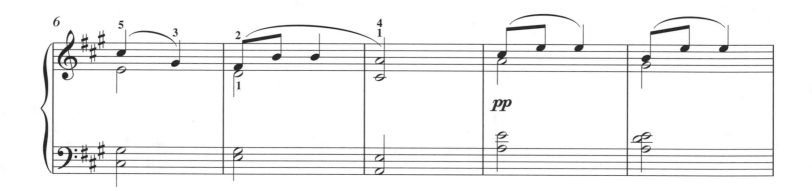

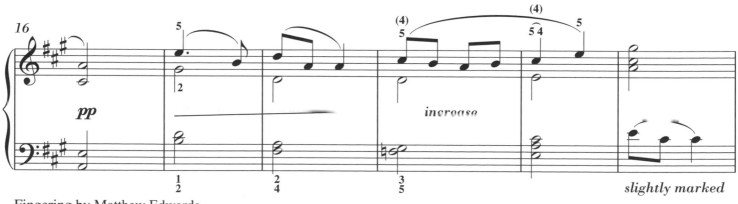

Fingering by Matthew Edwards.

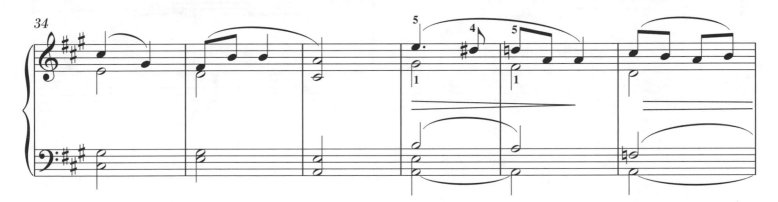

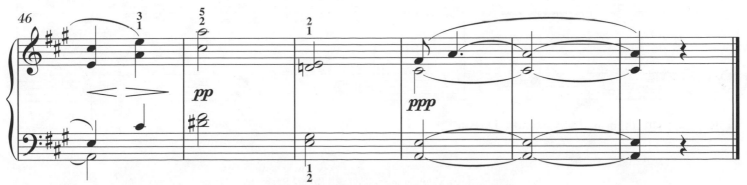

Mazurka in D minor
from *Album for the Young*

Pyotr Il'yich Tchaikovsky
Op. 39, No. 11

Не очень скоро (темп мазурки) [Not very fast (Mazurka tempo)] (♩. = 45–50)

Edited and with fingering by Alexandre Dossin.

Grandmother Tells a Ghost Story
from *Scenes from Childhood*

Theodor Kullak
Op. 81, No. 3

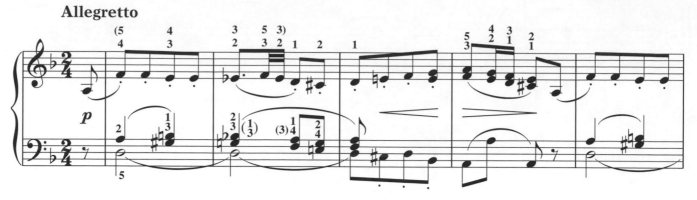

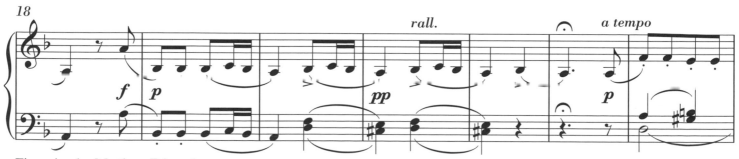

Fingering by Matthew Edwards.

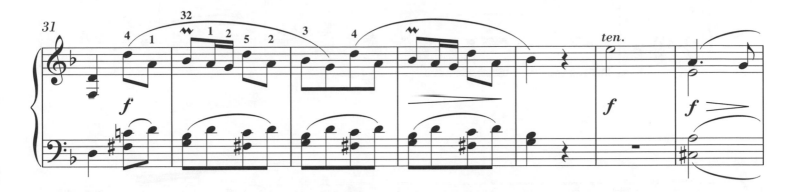

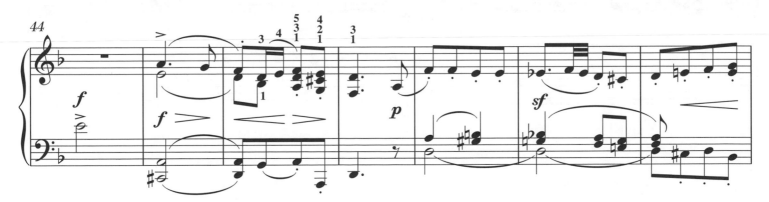

Grandmother
goes to sleep.

On the Playground
from *Scenes from Childhood*

Theodor Kullak
Op. 62, No. 4

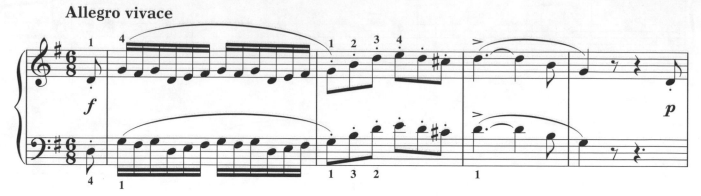

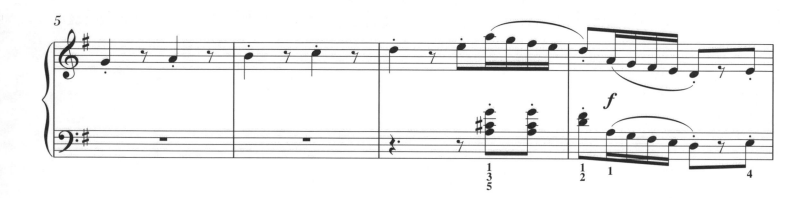

Fingering by Matthew Edwards.

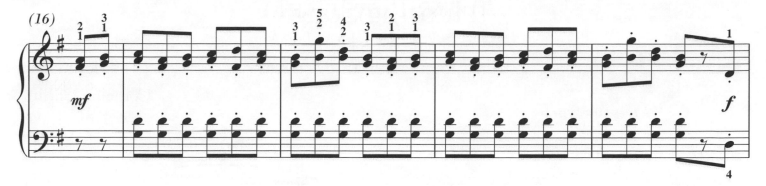

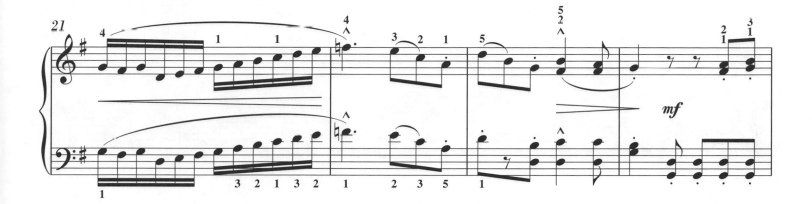

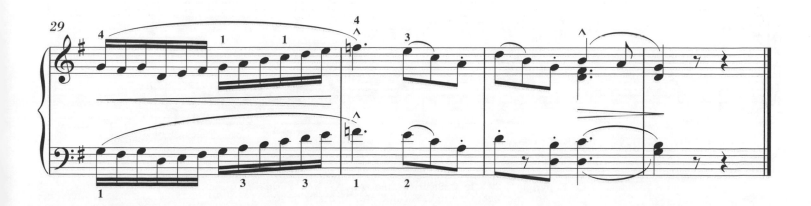

Hunting Song
(Jagdstück)
from *Albumleaves for the Young*

Cornelius Gurlitt
Op. 101, No. 19

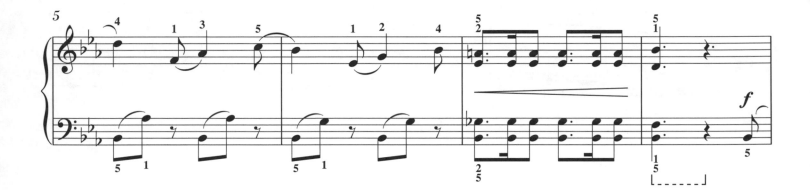

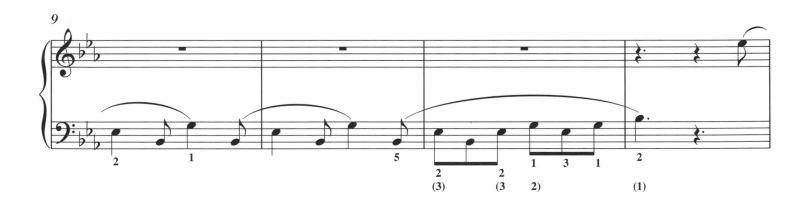

Edited and with fingering by Margaret Otwell.

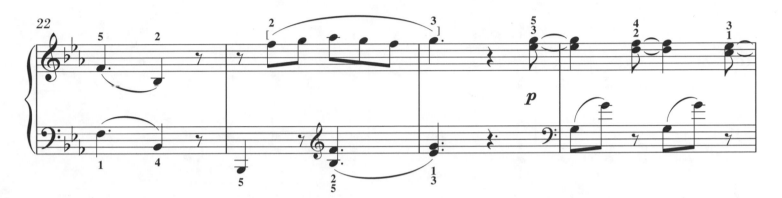

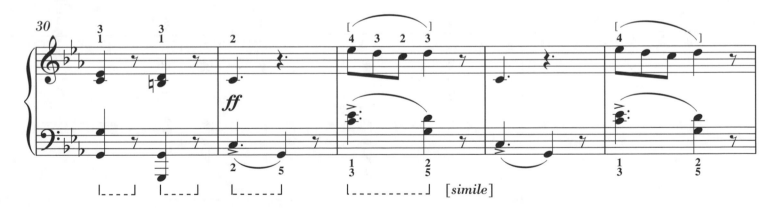

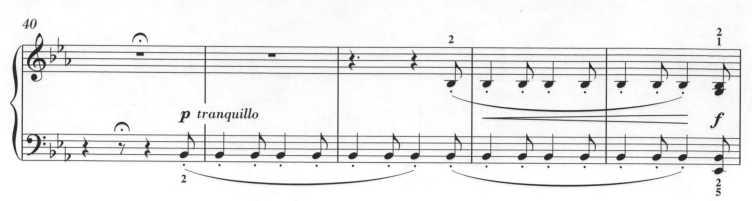

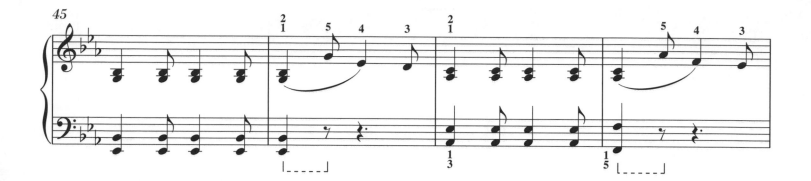

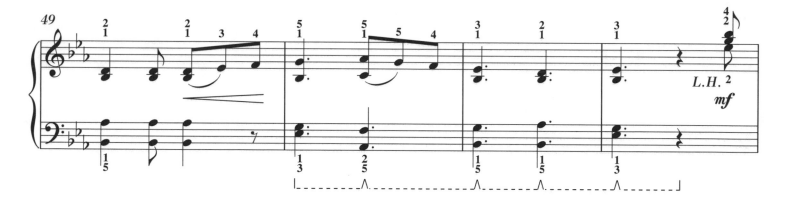

The Little Wanderer

(Der kleine Wandersmann)

from *Albumleaves for the Young*

Cornelius Gurlitt
Op. 101, No. 12

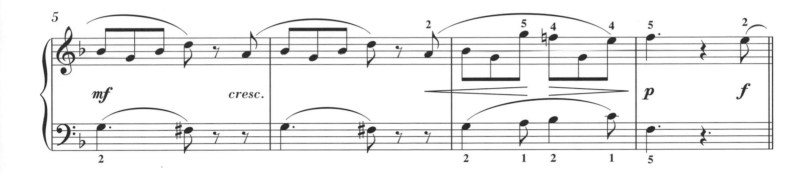

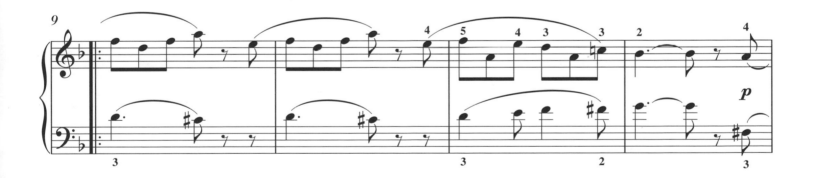

Edited and with fingering by Margaret Otwell.

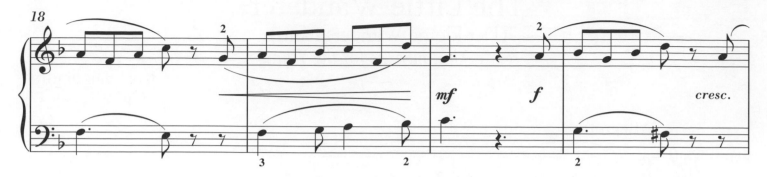

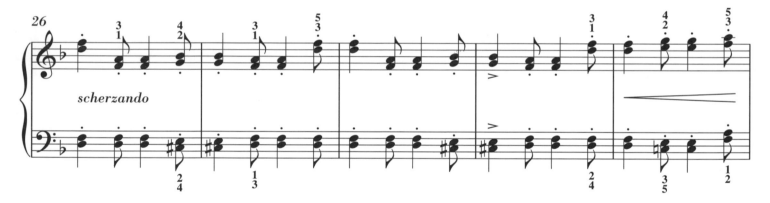

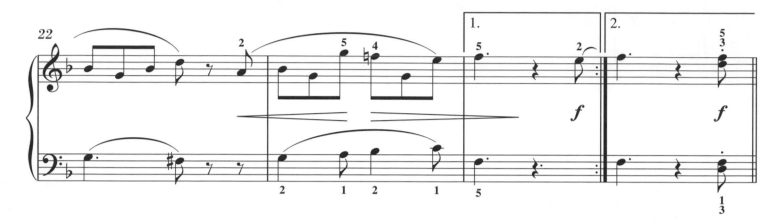

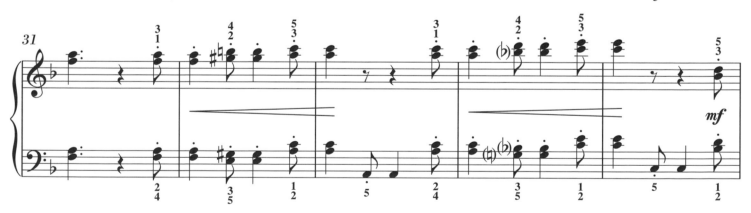

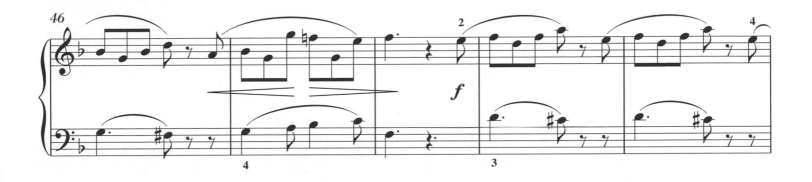

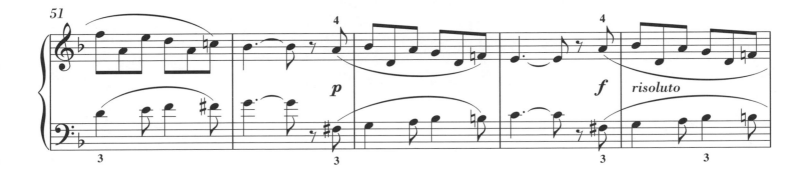

Hunting Song
(Jägerliedchen)
from *Album for the Young*

Robert Schumann
Op. 68, No. 7

Frisch und fröhlich
Briskly and merrily

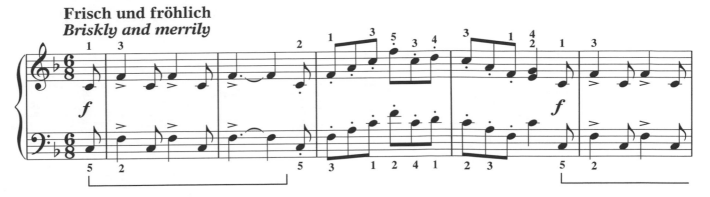

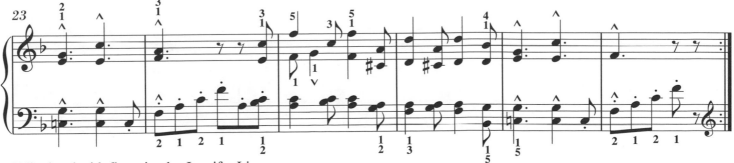

Edited and with fingering by Jennifer Linn.

Restlessness
(Inquiétude)
from *25 Progressive Studies*

Johann Friedrich Burgmüller
Op. 100, No. 18

Allegro agitato (♩ = 138)

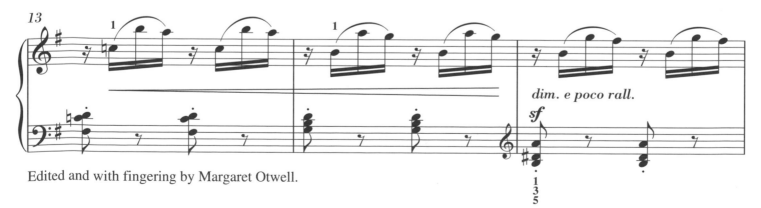

Edited and with fingering by Margaret Otwell.

The Dead Little Bird

from *Album for Young People*

Max Reger
Op. 17, No. 4

Andante espressivo

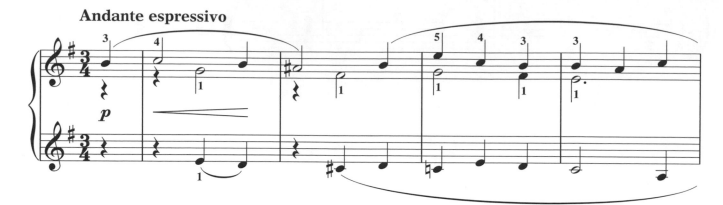

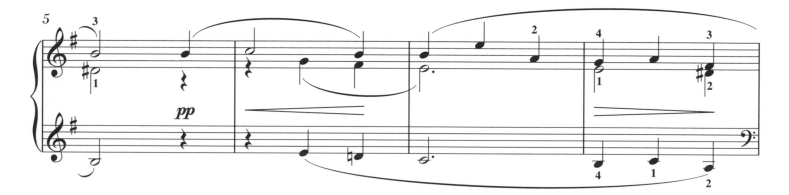

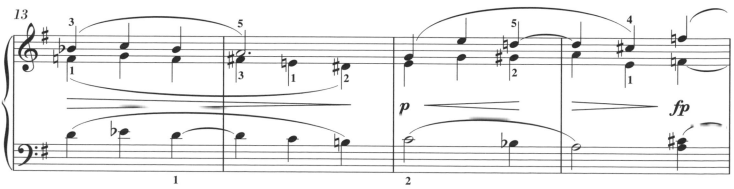

Fingering by Matthew Edwards.

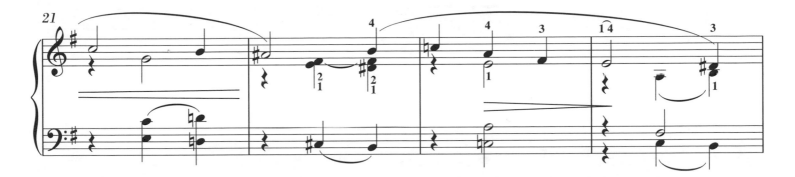

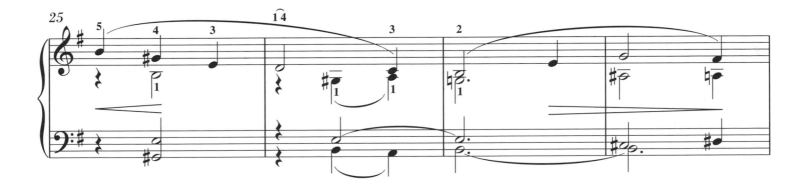

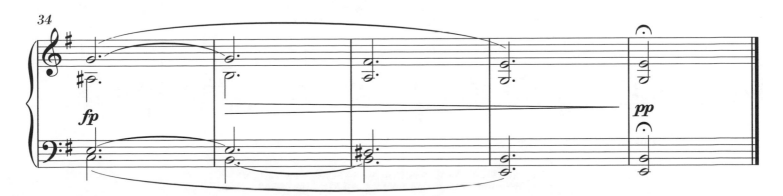

The Wooden Soldiers' March

from *Album for the Young*

Pyotr Il'yich Tchaikovsky
Op. 39, No. 5

Умеренно [Moderate] (♩ = 105–115)

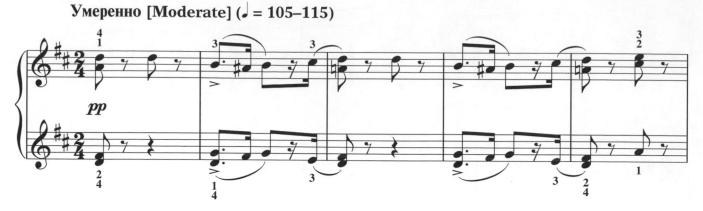

Edited and with fingering by Alexandre Dossin.

Gentle Complaint
(Douce Plainte)
from *25 Progressive Studies*

Johann Friedrich Burgmüller
Op. 100, No. 16

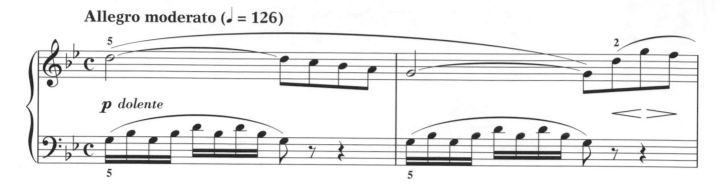

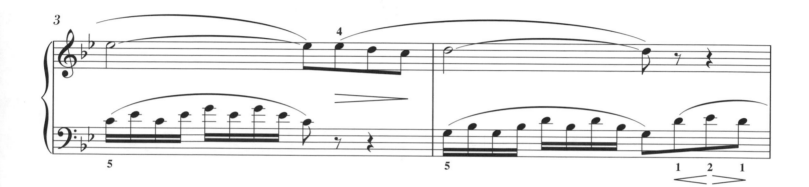

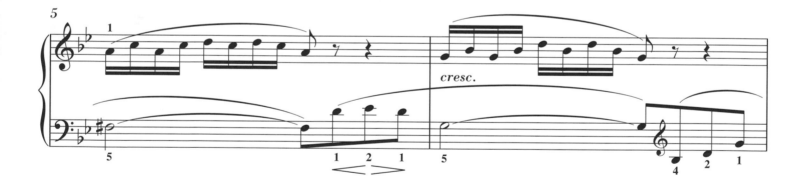

Edited and with fingering by Margaret Otwell.

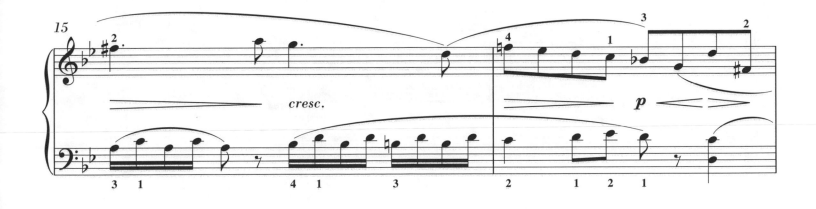

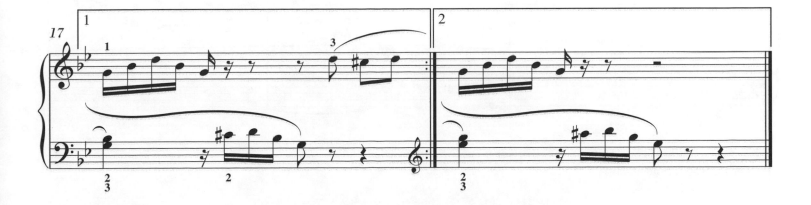

Folk Melody
from *Five Piano Pieces*

Carl Nielsen
Op. 3, No. 1

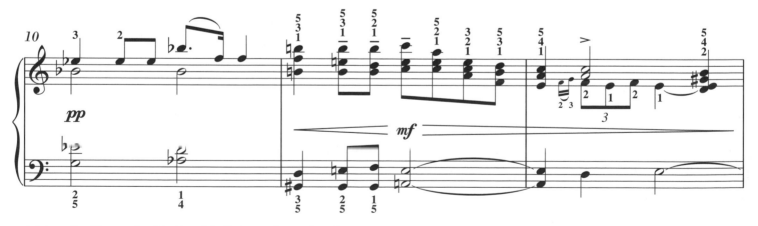

* Literally "humming" in Danish. It is unclear what the composer intends.
Fingering by Stefanie Jacob

Of Strange Lands and People
(Von fremden Ländern und Menschen)
from *Scenes from Childhood*

Robert Schumann
Op. 15, No. 1

Edited and with fingering by Jeffrey Biegel.

Sweet Dream
from *Album for the Young*

Pyotr Il'yich Tchaikovsky
Op. 39, No. 21

Edited and with fingering by Alexandre Dossin.

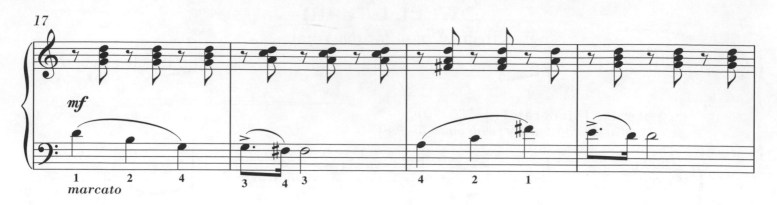

Study in A minor
(The Avalanche)
from *25 Melodious Etudes*

Stephen Heller
Op. 45, No. 2

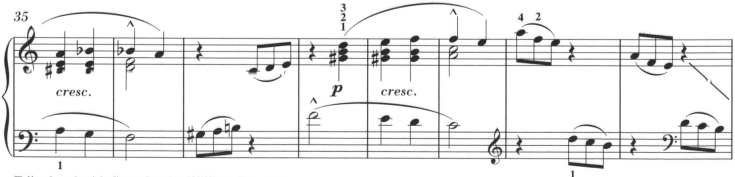

Edited and with fingering by William Westney.

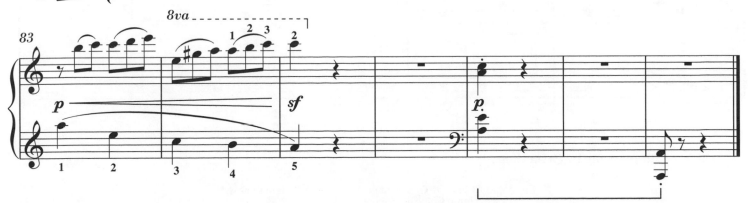

Prelude in A Major

Frédéric Chopin
Op. 28, No. 7

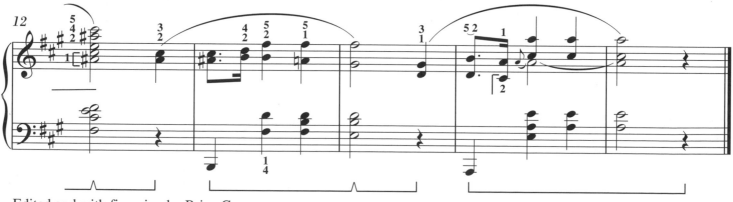

Edited and with fingering by Brian Ganz.

Little Romance
(Kleine Romanze)
from *Album for the Young*

Robert Schumann
Op. 68, No. 19

Edited and with fingering by Jennifer Linn.

Waltz in A minor
from *Lyric Pieces*

Edvard Grieg
Op. 12, No. 2

Edited and with fingering by William Westney.

*One might consider omitting the initial C-sharp from the left-hand chord in measures 39 and 47.

Confidence
from *18 Characteristic Studies*

Johann Friedrich Burgmüller
Op. 109, No. 1

Allegro non troppo [♩ = 144]

Edited and with fingering by William Westney.

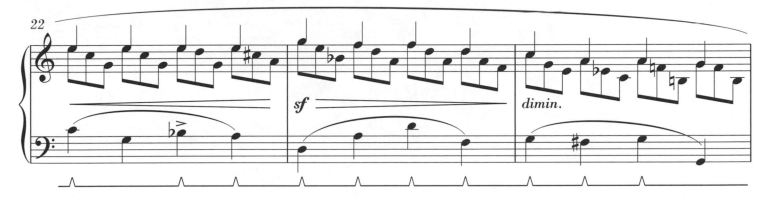

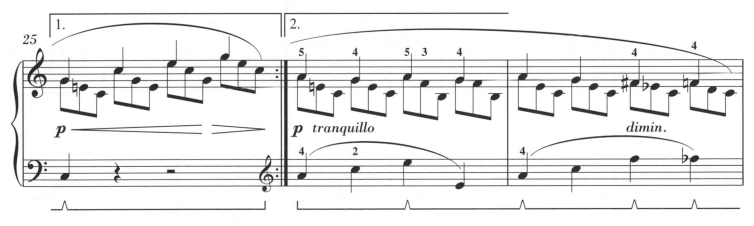

Arietta
from *Lyric Pieces*

Edvard Grieg
Op. 12, No. 1

Poco andante e sostenuto [♩ = 63–69]

Edited and with fingering by William Westney.

Dance of the Elves
from *Lyric Pieces*

Edvard Grieg
Op. 12, No. 4

Molto allegro e sempre staccato [♩. = 92–96]

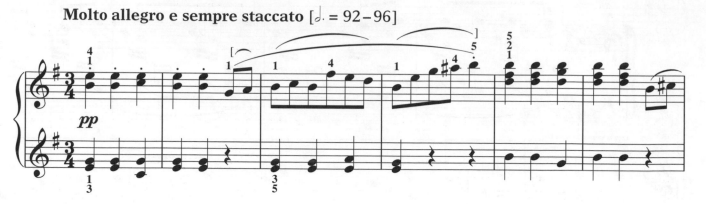

Edited and with fingering by William Westney.

Prelude in B minor

Frédéric Chopin
Op. 28, No. 6

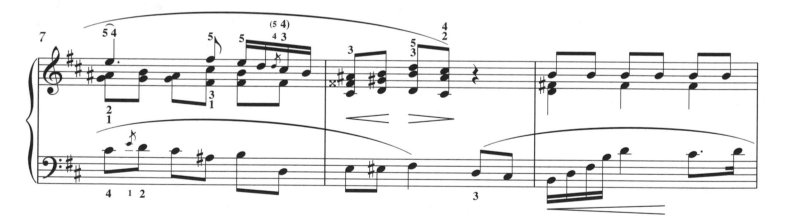

Edited and with fingering by Brian Ganz.

Puck
from *Lyric Pieces*

Edvard Grieg
Op. 71, No. 3

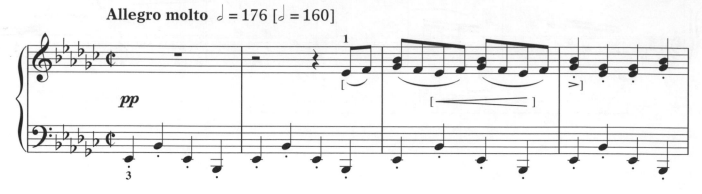

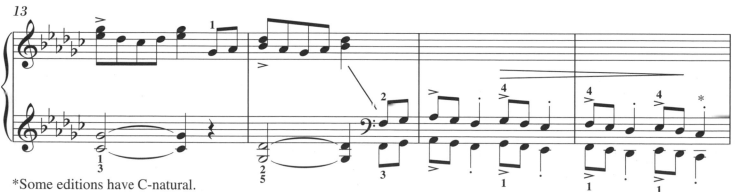

*Some editions have C-natural.
Edited and with fingering by William Westney.

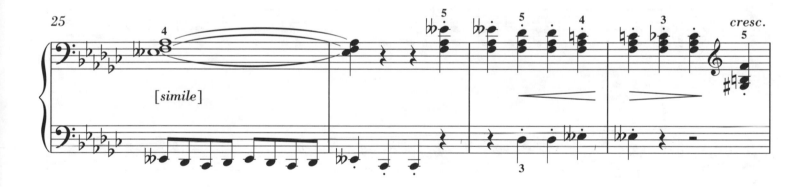

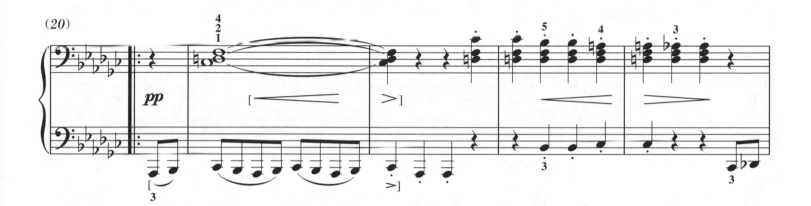

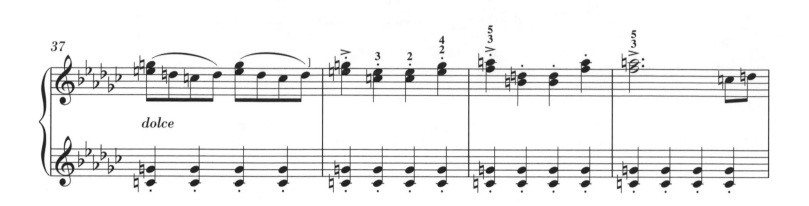

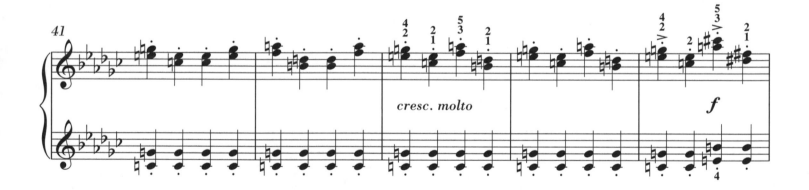

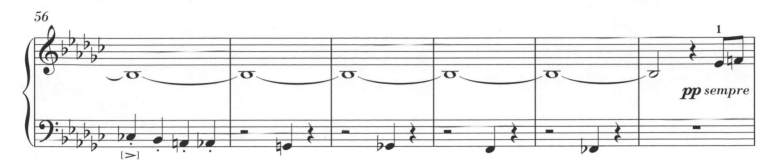

Little Neapolitan Song

from *Album for the Young*

Pyotr Il'yich Tchaikovsky
Op. 39, No. 18

Edited and with fingering by Alexandre Dossin.

Скоро [Fast] (♩ = 132–140)

Prelude in E minor

Frédéric Chopin
Op. 28, No. 4

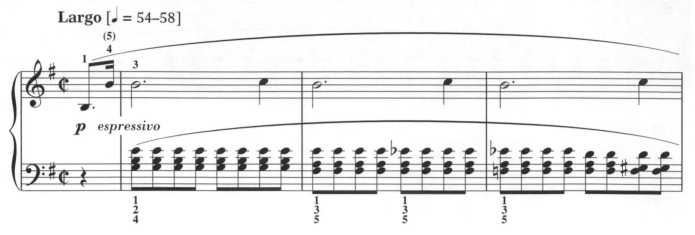

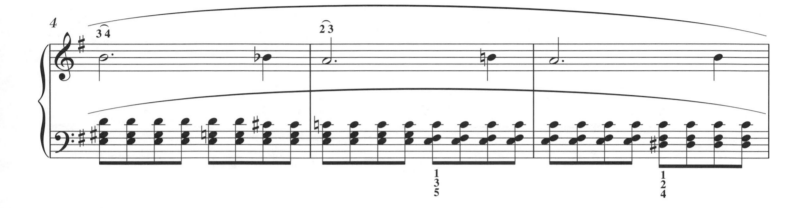

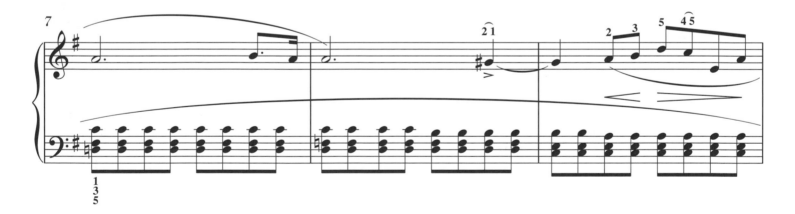

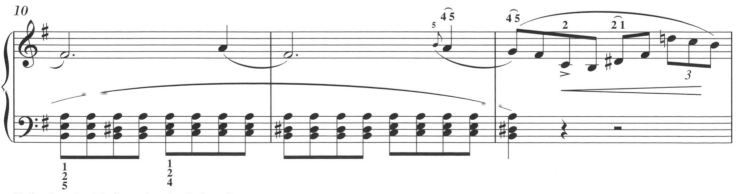

Edited and with fingering by Brian Ganz.

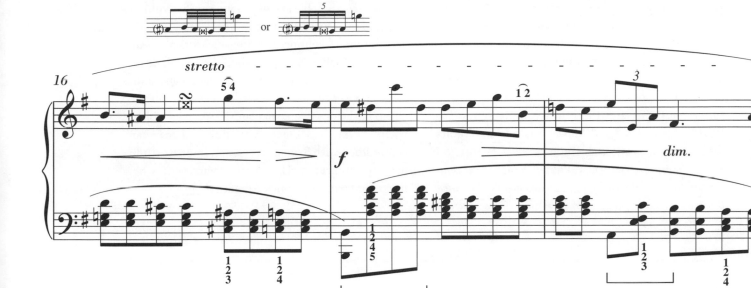

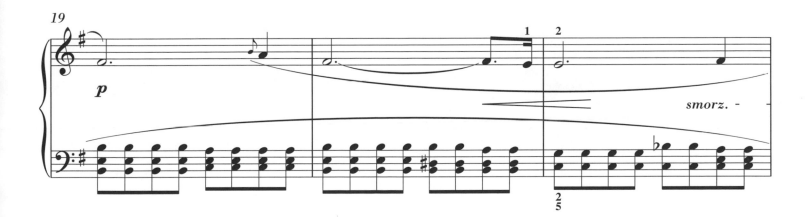

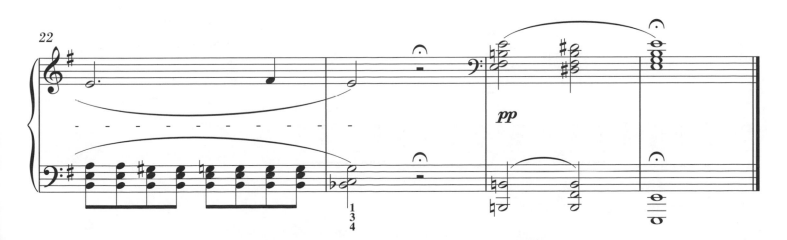

ABOUT THE EDITOR

RICHARD WALTERS

Richard Walters is a pianist, composer, and editor of hundred of publications in a long music publishing career. He is Vice President of Classical Publications at Hal Leonard, and directs a variety of publications for piano, voice, and solo instruments. Walters directs all publishing in the Schirmer Performance Editions series. Among other piano publications, he is editor of the revised edition of *Samuel Barber: Complete Piano Music, Leonard Bernstein: Music for Piano*, and the multi-volume series *The World's Great Classical Music*. His editing credits for vocal publications include *Samuel Barber: 65 Songs, Benjamin Britten: Collected Songs, Benjamin Britten: Complete Folksong Arrangements, Leonard Bernstein: Art Songs and Arias, The Purcell Collection: Realizations by Benjamin Britten, Bernstein Theatre Songs, G. Schirmer Collection of American Art Song, 28 Italian Songs and Arias for the Seventeenth and Eighteenth Centuries*, 80 volumes of standard repertoire in the Vocal Library series, and the multi-volume *The Singer's Musical Theatre Anthology*. Walters has published dozens of various arrangements, particularly for voice and piano, and is the composer of nine song cycles. He was educated with a bachelor's degree in piano at Simpson College, where he studied piano with Robert Larsen and composition with Sven Lekberg, and graduate studies in composition at the University of Minnesota, where he studied with Dominick Argento.